CONTENTS

Chapter 1 Bereavement and Loss

Chapter 2 Grief and Young People

Chapter 3 Handling the Formalities

OTHER TITLES IN THE ISSUES SERIES

For more on these titles, visit: www.independence.co.uk

EXPLORING THE ISSUES

Photocopiable study guides to accompany the above publications. Each four-page A4 guide provides a variety of discussion points and other activities to suit a wide range of ability levels and interests.

A note on critical evaluation

Because the information reprinted here is from a number of different sources, readers should bear in mind the origin of the text and whether the source is likely to have a particular bias when presenting information (just as they would if undertaking their own research). It is hoped that, as you read about the many aspects of the issues explored in this book, you will critically evaluate the information presented. It is important that you decide whether you are being presented with facts or opinions. Does the writer give a biased or an unbiased report? If an opinion is being expressed, do you agree with the writer?

Bereavement and Grief offers a useful starting point for those who need convenient access to information about the many issues involved. However, it is only a starting point. Following each article is a URL to the relevant organisation's website, which you may wish to visit for further information.

Bereavement and Grief

Lisa Firth

Independence

Educational Publishers

Cambridge

First published by Independence

The Studio, High Green

Great Shelford

Cambridge CB22 5EG

England

© Independence 2010

Photocopy licence

The material in this book is protected by copyright. However, the
purchaser is free to make multiple copies of particular articles for instructional
purposes for immediate use within the purchasing institution.
Making copies of the entire book is not permitted.

British Library Cataloguing in Publication Data

Bereavement and grief. -- (Issues ; v. 192)

1. Bereavement. 2. Bereavement in adolescence. 3. Death.

I. Series II. Firth, Lisa.

155.9'37-dc22

ISBN-13: 978 1 86168 543 8

Printed in Great Britain

MWL Print Group Ltd

Bereavement: key facts

Information from the Royal College of Psychiatrists.

Bereavement

Bereavement is our experience of grief when someone we care about has died.

It isn't just one feeling but a range of different emotions. We feel them most in the months – often up to two years, sometimes longer – after the death.

After this, although life is very different, most people manage to come to terms with their loss.

We most often grieve for someone that we have known for some time. But if you have had a stillbirth, or miscarriage, or have lost a very young baby, you will go through many of the same emotions.

What feelings am I likely to have?

There is no 'standard' way of grieving. Cultures and individuals have their own beliefs and ceremonies. However, they all share many experiences.

You might feel:

Numb: Particularly in the few hours or days following the death, you feel simply stunned, as though you can't believe it has actually happened.

Agitated: After a few days the numbness usually wears off. You feel a sense of agitation, of pining or yearning for the dead person. You want somehow to find them, even though you know you can't. You find it difficult to relax, concentrate or sleep properly. You may dream, see fleeting visions or hear the voice of your loved one.

Angry: You can feel very angry – towards doctors and nurses who did not prevent the death, towards friends and relatives who did not do enough, or even towards the person who has died because they have gone.

Guilty: You may find yourself going over all the things you would have liked to have said or done. You may wonder if you could have prevented the death, even though death is usually beyond anyone's control.

Relieved: You may feel relieved if your loved one has died after a painful or distressing illness. This is not callous – it is common and understandable.

Sad: After the weeks of strong feelings, you may gradually become quietly sad and withdrawn. You feel less agitated but experience more periods of depression. These peak between four and six weeks later.

Reflective: For several months, other people may see you as spending a lot of time just sitting, doing nothing. In fact, you are thinking about the person you have lost, going over in your mind your memories of the times you had together. This is a quiet, but essential part of coming to terms with the death.

You are becoming whole again: As time passes, the fierce pain of early bereavement fades, the sadness lifts and you start to think about other things and look to the future. Although the sense of having lost a part of yourself never goes away entirely, after some time you can feel whole again.

Like letting go: You finally 'let go' of the person who has died and start a new sort of life. The sadness lifts, you sleep better, start to feel more energetic and may find that your sexual feelings now return.

What if I can't come to terms with it?

⇨ You may have problems if you can't grieve properly at the time of your loss because of family or business commitments. Some people don't appear to grieve at all and return quickly to their normal life but then, years later, have odd physical symptoms or spells of depression.

⇨ If you have had a stillbirth, miscarriage or abortion, other people may not understand why you feel so deeply about it. This can make you feel very alone and low.

⇨ You may start to grieve, but get stuck. The early sense of shock and disbelief goes on. Years may pass and still you find it hard to believe that the person you loved is dead.

⇨ You may find that you can't think of anything else, perhaps making the room of the dead person into a shrine.

⇨ Occasionally, you may feel so low that you have thoughts of killing yourself and may even stop eating and drinking.

⇨ Bereavement can affect your physical health, with an increased risk of cancer and heart disease. Some older people may die very soon after their partner or spouse has died.

What help can I get?

If you find it hard to come to terms with the loss of a loved one, voluntary or religious organisations may be able to help. Meeting and talking to people who have been through the same experience might be enough. If not, you might want to see a bereavement counsellor or psychotherapist, in a group or on your own. Your GP can help you to find one.

If you can't sleep for a while, sleeping tablets from your doctor may help – but only for a few days. If the depression gets worse, affecting your appetite, energy and sleep, your GP should be able to arrange counselling or antidepressants. If the depression gets worse, despite treatment, you may need to see a psychiatrist.

How can I help someone else?

⇨ Spend time with the bereaved person so they feel less alone with their grief.

⇨ Let them, if they want to, cry with you and talk about their feelings.

⇨ Don't tell them to pull themselves together.

⇨ Help out with practical things.

⇨ Try to be around at particularly painful times, such as anniversaries.

⇨ Give them time to grieve.

⇨ Information from the Royal College of Psychiatrists. Visit www.rcpsych.ac.uk for more information.

© *Royal College of Psychiatrists*

Bereavement – what you can do to help yourself

Tips to help you through a loss.

⇨ Accept that it isn't unusual not to feel your 'normal' self. Be gentle with yourself for grief is an exhausting thing.

⇨ Let yourself experience the feelings you have about what has happened and talk to others about it – over and over again if you need to.

⇨ Write down all the feelings that are going around in your head, especially before going to bed as this may help you sleep better.

⇨ You may need to find out more about what happened if all the facts are not clear about how your loved one died. Sometimes you will never know.

⇨ Some return to routine can help as long as you try to balance this with time to reflect on what has happened to you. Try sticking to a regular routine of eating, sleeping, exercise and relaxation.

⇨ Look after yourself. Your self-esteem may have taken a real knock. Acknowledge yourself each time you achieve something, even if it is getting up in the morning or staying in bed to give yourself a rest. We can be very good at noticing all our mistakes and ignoring our good points, especially when we are feeling down.

⇨ Remembering happy times with the person who has died can be painful but nonetheless healing. Looking at photographs, making a memory book and keeping meaningful mementoes may help.

⇨ Take things slowly. You might want to delay making big changes such as moving house, starting a new relationship or changing job. You have already suffered a huge loss and need to adjust to that first.

⇨ The above information is reprinted with kind permission from ParentlinePlus, the UK's leading charity providing free, confidential support for parents and families.

Parentline: 0808 800 2222

Email: parentsupport@parentlineplus.org.uk

Website: www.parentlineplus.org.uk.

© *ParentlinePlus*

Coping with your grief

Information from Marie Curie Cancer Care.

Grieving is a natural process that can take place after any kind of loss. Dealing with loss can be very distressing but it is normal – albeit very difficult and painful – to experience very strong reactions. Grief is not an illness. Your feelings are something you experience and not symptoms that have to be treated.

Look after yourself physically. Try to eat well and get plenty of rest. It is very easy to overlook your physical needs when you are busy dealing with everything that has to be done after a death, or struggling with grief.

Everyone grieves in their own way

Everyone reacts in their own way when they are grieving for someone who was very close to them. Each person and relationship is special and unique. Don't worry if you're not reacting the way other people seem to be, or if someone says you should be feeling or behaving a certain way and you're not. The important thing is to allow yourself to feel and do what is right for you in your own time.

Take your time to make choices

Your first reaction may include disbelief and confusion. You may find it impossible to take in what has happened. Even if you were expecting a person to die, the moment of death may have come as a shock, leaving you feeling unprepared and anxious or even angry.

There will be some practical things to attend to and decisions to make. Some things do have to be done quickly, but don't feel you have to rush into decisions if there is no need. Think about what you really want and take your time. You may find it helpful to talk to someone about practical issues. Don't enter into any financial or legal agreements unless you fully understand them and don't let others rush you into anything before you are ready.

Intense feelings are part of grieving

People often find that the first two or three months after someone has died are quite busy with practical things to attend to. It can be after this period that the full impact of your loss may be felt.

You may be surprised by the intensity of your feelings. You may become forgetful and find it hard to concentrate. You may experience a whole range of feelings including physical pain and great sadness, isolation, helplessness, anxiety, relief and anger that the person has died.

You may be angry at yourself because you wish you had done things differently and now feel you have no opportunity to put things right and be forgiven. You may be angry at the person for dying. You may be angry at the world for your loss, or feel anger towards your god.

It is not uncommon to feel relief that the person has died and then feel guilty about feeling this way. There may be many different reasons why you would have such feelings – situations and relationships can be very complicated – but try not to feel guilty because they are also part of grieving.

You may also find that feelings return about a previous loss which you thought you were over, or that you now grieve for a previous loss that didn't seem to affect you at the time.

Grief is not an illness. Your feelings are something you experience and not symptoms that have to be treated

Don't hide your feelings. Do express them as much as possible and talk to someone you trust. You may find you need to talk through your feelings repeatedly.

Don't ignore your grief or try to move on before you feel ready. There is no right or wrong amount of time to grieve. Recovery is not a constant process – sometimes you will feel worse rather than better, but this is normal. You may also find that birthdays, holidays and anniversaries are difficult times, even when you thought you had moved on.

You may find it helpful to make some longer-term plans so that you have something to look forward to in the future.

Grieving within a family

Your family and friends will also be experiencing grief which will be unique to them. It can be upsetting if one family member feels very angry while another feels intense sadness and needs to cry, or if one person needs to talk about their feelings while another wants to say very little.

Try to acknowledge these differences. Sharing your thoughts and feelings can lessen the loneliness and bring you closer together.

MARIE CURIE CANCER CARE

Including children

Generally, children under four or five years old do not understand that a person who has died will not come back. Children and young people often need to be reminded of this again and again.

Children experience the passage of time differently from adults and can therefore appear to overcome grief quite quickly.

However, children in their early school years may need reassuring that they are not responsible for the death of a close friend or relative as they often blame themselves for one reason or another.

This is something that anyone who is bereaved may experience, but it is particularly common for this age group.

If you are caring for grieving children, it is important to share your grief. Even very young children experience grief and need to be given the opportunity to express their feelings. You may want to protect your child from the pain of grief but, as one mother said: 'It isn't a choice of whether she will hurt or not but whether I will know about it.'

Children often know more than adults realise and they need honest information to help them make sense of what has happened. If you are unsure about how to support your child then it may be helpful to talk to your GP, health visitor or practice nurse.

Some Marie Curie Hospices have Children and Young People's Workers who may be able to offer advice and support. All our hospices can provide you with booklets about helping children.

Where to go for support

During the coming weeks and months you may need help and support from others – it can be very hard to manage bereavement alone. If you are worried about your feelings, it may also help to talk them through. Asking for help is not a sign of weakness; it takes courage and strength.

Many people find that their close family and friends are a tremendous help, so do make sure you keep in touch with them. Even if they themselves are grieving, they may want to be close to you to support and care for you.

Within your circle of family and friends, you may find that someone isn't as supportive as you might have expected or hoped. For instance, perhaps they seem to avoid you, or change the subject whenever you mention your loss or your feelings.

Everyone reacts differently to another person's grief just as everyone reacts differently to their own loss. It may be that they simply don't know what to say, or are worried that if they mention the subject they will upset you. It can be very difficult for someone who hasn't experienced bereavement to understand how strongly it can affect you, or to realise just how long you will be affected. On the other hand, perhaps it brings back memories of a loss of their own so they are too distressed to talk about the subject at all. Perhaps they feel the need to fix things or do something when there's nothing that can be done or fixed at the moment.

If someone isn't supportive in the way you need, it doesn't mean they don't care about you. There may be many different reasons for their reaction. If you feel an important relationship is being affected by this, you could raise the issue or ask a trusted third party to do so.

Children under four or five years old do not understand that a person who has died will not come back

---

Alternatively, you may decide to look to them for a different type of support. For instance, someone who doesn't feel comfortable discussing how you feel may be delighted to provide practical support such as babysitting or helping with a DIY job. Or someone who feels they have to do something or 'fix' things may be reassured that simply listening to you can help while other actions aren't necessary (and might not help at this point).

Sometimes you may have to leave the issue unresolved – or deal with it when your loss is further behind you.

It may also help to talk to someone outside your family and circle of friends. You could contact someone else who you trust – a minister of religion, or your GP or practice nurse. They should be able to recommend a local bereavement support group or counsellor.

If the person who has died was cared for by a Marie Curie Hospice, the hospice will contact you within eight weeks of the death to offer you bereavement support. However, if you would like support sooner, do not hesitate to contact the hospice. Most Marie Curie Hospices have social workers, chaplains, a family bereavement support team or other bereavement support services for advice and information.

If the person who has died was cared for by another local hospice, try contacting the hospice to see what support or information they can offer. They may recommend other support services in the area.

⇨ Information from Marie Curie Cancer Care. Visit www.mariecurie.org.uk for more information.

© Marie Curie Cancer Care

Helping the bereaved

Many people find coping with bereaved family and friends an awkward and difficult time. Everyone knows the stories of people who would rather cross the street than face what they feel would be a potentially embarrassing conversation with someone who has been recently bereaved.

Make contact

It is very important to make contact as soon as possible. Contact the bereaved person immediately to tell them how sorry you are to hear of their loss. Send a letter or card and flowers if appropriate. Most bereaved people say that reading the letters and cards they receive provides valuable support and comfort, particularly during the many sleepless nights they endure. You may worry that your words seem rather banal or trite, but they often take on a deeper significance and offer a degree of consolation in the heightened emotions of bereavement.

Maintain contact

Keep the contact going with visits, phone calls and letters, particularly as the weeks and months pass by. Often levels of support can fall away in the months after a bereavement, but this is the time when the bereaved can be the loneliest and most vulnerable. Six months is recognised as being a particularly vulnerable time, as it is about this time that the reality of the loss hits home and yet others are assuming that by this stage, people are over the worst. Continue to invite them to events and functions which you would have previously. They can always say no, but don't make that assumption yourself.

Listen and let the bereaved person talk

Talking is recognised as one of the most important elements in the grieving and healing process. Let the bereaved person talk about the person who has died and don't be embarrassed by their tears and anger. Don't use platitudes – Kate Boydell in her excellent website www.merrywidow.me.uk says, 'People use platitudes as a replacement for personal experiences, substituting insensitivity for insight. If in doubt, don't say it.'

Talk about the person who has died

Many people feel that they shouldn't talk about the person that has died as this will bring on another wave of grief. However most bereaved people say that they find it hurtful if the deceased is not mentioned, almost as if they had never existed. Remember happy times, things they liked or didn't like, funny things they said. It all helps to keep the memories strong and bring some comfort.

Offer practical help

Consider what practical support you can offer, such as taking a cooked meal, taking care of the children, shopping or helping with any funeral arrangements. Try and maintain regular help for as long as needed or possible but try not to make promises that you will not be able to keep. Don't say 'Give me a call if you need anything', help needs to be freely given without the bereaved person having to ask for it – make regular contact and make a date to have the bereaved person/family around for a coffee or Sunday lunch; take the children out; make an extra cake/casserole and drop it round.

Muslim tradition requires that mourners do not cook for themselves for 40 days after a death – relatives and neighbours supply the food.

Be aware of significant dates and anniversaries

Family times such as Christmas and birthdays as well as anniversaries of the death are a particularly difficult and traumatic time for the bereaved and need to be treated with sensitivity, particularly the first few times they come around.

Helping children

Once adults tried to shield children from death, but modern-day understanding is that avoidance is a recipe for disaster – especially for a child. Like all of us, children need to understand that death is a natural part of life, just as birth is and two charities in particular are very able to help children, parents and families through the grieving process with professional carers, helpful publications and activities.

Contact The Child Bereavement Trust and Winston's Wish, for example.

Widowhood – A Young Woman's Survival Guide can be found on Kate Boydell's wonderful website – www. merrywidow.me.uk

Kate was widowed at the age of 33 with two young children and her personal experience offers a highly practical, painfully poignant and at time, amusing insight into the emotions and experiences of widowhood, from telling her children the news, to coping with DIY.

This is a valuable resource for everyone and is equally

IFISHOULDDIE.CO.UK

useful for those trying to help and understand bereaved family and friends.

Helpful reading

Waterbugs and Dragonflies by Doris Stickney – Continuum International Publishing Group – Mowbray/August 1997

Specially aimed at children, it helps to explain death through the analogy of the waterbugs' short life under water and their emergence as dragonflies as the human's life after death.

⇨ The above information is reprinted with kind permission from ifishoulddie.co.uk. Visit www.ifishoulddie.co.uk for more information.

Grief before death

Information from NHS Choices.

Carers often feel grief even though the person they're caring for is still alive. This could happen if the person being cared for has a life-limiting condition (a condition that has no reasonable hope of a cure), or their personality has been affected by their illness.

Although not everyone experiences this 'anticipatory grief', people who do can feel the same emotions and sense of mourning as if the person had actually died.

You may have a wide range of emotions, such as loss, dread, guilt and anxiety. Everyone reacts differently, and it's good to accept that your coping method is unique.

The grief you might experience may not initially be for the person you care for, but for the life you currently lead. Becoming a carer can change your life dramatically, and you may feel like you've lost some of your freedom or social life.

The extra responsibility, and not being able to do anything without planning, can be stressful. You might feel guilty about feeling this way, but it's a natural reaction to such a big change in your life.

Grieving before a person dies doesn't necessarily mean that you won't grieve when they pass away. Everyone reacts differently to these circumstances. While some people feel prepared for the death and have closure, others may start the grieving process all over again.

Dealing with conditions that affect a person's personality and memory can be very traumatic, particularly if you're caring for a relative or close friend.

Many carers find that they grieve for the loss of the person they once were. You might grieve for the memories that you have together, which the cared-for person will forget. You may grieve for the changes to their personality or for any future plans that they may no longer be able to carry out. You may feel conflicting emotions as the person you look after loses their mental functions or stops recognising you.

Knowing that others are going through the same experience can be helpful. Many carers have taken comfort from an interview for *ITN News* earlier this year in which former newsreader John Suchet discussed his feelings of loss after his wife was diagnosed with dementia.

Terminal conditions

Finding out that someone you care for has a terminal disease can leave you feeling powerless and devastated.

If you experience pre-death grief, it's just as vital for you to talk to someone and feel supported as it is when someone has already died. You might find that it helps to talk to friends and family, or the person you care for. It's not uncommon for the person with the condition to experience anticipatory grief, so you may find comfort in talking to each other.

You might also consider talking to a counsellor. It can help to discuss your feelings with someone who is objective and doesn't have emotional ties to the situation. This can help, particularly if the person you care for is in denial about their condition. The counsellor can talk to you about your feelings, suggest ways that you can help the person being cared for, and discuss the difficult post-death decisions that you may need to make, such as organ donation.

Bottling up your emotions can leave you feeling overwhelmed and, in some cases, affect your health. So it's important to find someone to support you.

Last reviewed 14 September 2009

⇨ Reproduced from NHS Choices with permission. For more information, please visit the NHS Choices website at www.nhs.uk

A stiff upper lip is no longer a badge of honour

For generations public grief has embarrassed Britain. But as a new generation experiences the pain of war, that is changing.

By Ben Macintyre

A wave of bitter collective grief is beginning to break across the land of the stiff upper lip. You can sense it every time another funeral cortège wends through Wootton Bassett. You could feel in the subdued crowd that packed Whitehall on Remembrance Sunday.

You can see it in the tired eyes not just of the newly bereaved widow and her frightened children, but also of those turning out in their support, and of those writing and reporting on it. Mourning is exhausting.

This upsurge of public grief has not happened simply because Remembrance Day coincided with a savage rise in the death toll in Afghanistan. It does not merely reflect ebbing support for the war, anger over our political leaders, or uncertainty about our war aims.

It feels more elemental than that – a deep-tissue communal sadness, a sense of shared hopelessness that comes with the tragedy of sudden, violent death. This collective grieving happens quite rarely in British society, but when it does, its effects – social, cultural and, above all, political – can be profound.

Traditionally, Britons have disdained exhibitions of public emotion, particularly in wartime. Mass demonstrations of bereavement, whether for famous individuals, family or war dead, were seen as a sign of weakness. An entire empire was built on the ability to suppress emotion.

During and after the First World War, excessive public grieving was forbidden, bequeathing a poisonous legacy of unaddressed trauma. That war left about three million widows and six million orphans, but public anguish and protracted mourning were seen as unpatriotic.

An entire generation of combatants was encouraged to cauterise the wounds of memory. The response to the question 'What did you do in the Great War, Daddy?' was usually a gruff refusal to discuss it. Real grief was subsumed in the official trappings of heroic death: war memorials, statues, Kipling's restrained epitaphs and euphemism. The emotional reality of war was stifled.

The Second World War also discouraged the wearing of hearts on sleeves, particularly uniformed sleeves. The culture conspired to suppress overt mourning: if Noël Coward could show no emotion amid the carnage in *In Which We Serve*, so should everyone else. Grief was just collateral damage. 'Keep buggering on,' Winston Churchill ordered.

The turning point came with the death of Diana, Princess of Wales, which prompted an expression of mass grief unequalled in British history. Before her death the ability to suppress emotion was regarded as a virtue, restrained mourning a mark of decorum: exactly the qualities for which the Royal Family were pilloried. The grieving may have been extreme and exacerbated by crowd mentality, but it was undeniably authentic. The way we mourn changed for ever: today it is not only reasonable but cathartic publicly to mourn someone you have never met.

> **Grief is not easily put into words. It is more simply represented by ritual, wreath laying and hymn singing, flowers, candles, prayers and two minutes of silence**

Some dismiss the Diana effect as banal and meaningless, a 'new emotionalism' that allows strangers to wallow in mawkish sentimentality and piggy-back on the genuine bereavements of others. Some see the growth of public grieving for dead celebrities and murdered children as 'mourning sickness', driven less by real emotion than by the desire to be seen to care.

Mourning was once the preserve of the elderly. Today's public mourners are far younger, brought up in an atmosphere of emotional honesty and openness to collective grief. The crowds in Whitehall and yesterday in Trafalgar Square contain many of the Facebook generation, come to remember the dead of their own age after eight years of war.

Gordon Brown comes from a generation where mourning is private, but to demonstrate sympathy for the bereaved he has had to evoke the death of his own daughter.

Grief is not easily put into words. It is more simply represented by ritual, wreath laying and hymn singing, flowers, candles, prayers and two minutes of silence. But at a more profound level, mourning can simply mean turning up to stand with others similarly distressed.

This is what is happening, with increasing intensity at Wootton Bassett and throughout the country. There is solace in solidarity and comfort in crowds. And the

THE TIMES

crowds are growing. Most of the 2,000 people who turned out this week did not know the dead soldiers personally. This public mourning began spontaneously simply because the route from RAF Lyneham passes through the Wiltshire town, and has grown organically.

There is a medieval pilgrimage gene in our national make-up, and once again we are gathering to mourn. The Wootton Bassett crowds are primarily emotional, but are steadily becoming more political, in protest against the Government and the policy in Afghanistan, just as mourning Diana became focused into resentment towards the Royal Family.

Public grief for the dead of the Afghan war can be sentimental and manufactured but, in an age when we no longer fear emotion, it demonstrates a willingness to confront the true nature of war and death in a way that our ancestors in two world wars too often did not.

In 1996 I attended the 80th anniversary of the Battle of the Somme and met a man called Donald Hodge, then 101, who had gone over the top on the first day of the carnage. While the top brass spoke of courage and sacrifice, 80 years later, Mr Hodge was still grieving. 'I have so many friends who lie here,' he said. For someone of his generation to speak openly of his own grief was proof of a different sort of bravery.

A palpable sombreness hung over this year's Remembrance Day ritual, a collective sense of loss. Perhaps that is war frustration or political disillusionment, but it also shows how far we have come in acknowledging the painful and bloody reality of war, when a lip trembling in shared grief is a greater badge of honour than a stiff upper lip.

12 November 2009

Major new survey reveals people's reluctance to discuss own death

Information from Dying Matters.

New research, commissioned by the Dying Matters Coalition, shows that less than a third (29%) of people have discussed their wishes around dying and only 4% have written advance care plans, despite the fact that more than two thirds (68%) of people questioned say they are comfortable talking about death.

The research, undertaken by NatCen, examines public attitudes to a range of issues relating to death, dying and bereavement. It reveals that, while we have strong views about end of life, we are still unlikely to have discussed our own death, despite personal experience of issues related to dying. Currently 60% of people die in hospitals, yet the survey reveals that 70% of people would like to die at home, illustrating the importance of talking openly about our wishes if we want them to be met.

A carer talking to a member of the Dying Matters Coalition said:

'It's not easy to talk about end of life issues, but it's important to do. Now that we've put our affairs in order and are talking about what we want, we can "put that in a box" as it were, and get on with living one day at a time, cherishing each day together, as I know it's going to end one day.'

A bereaved wife said:

'If you talk about dying, you can say everything you want or need to. There are no regrets.'

Of those people who had not discussed any aspect of their end of life care, 45% felt it was because death feels a long way off, and a further 18% said they were too young to discuss it. 8% of 65- to 74-year-olds thought they were too young to discuss dying.

The new Dying Matters Coalition has been set up to raise awareness and to provide the support and information needed to have these conversations with loved ones. It aims to make dying well a natural part of a good life and through this help change attitudes and behaviours towards death, dying and bereavement. And through this raise the profile and improve end of life care.

Professor Mayur Lakhani, GP and Chair of Dying Matters Coalition, said:

'As a practising GP, I know that many people feel frightened to talk about death for fear of upsetting the person they love. However, it is essential that people do not leave it until it is too late. Planning for needs and wishes helps you to be in control, and it helps those we leave behind. A good life needs a good ending. This can be achieved by talking about it early on with relatives, friends or carers.'

10 February 2010

⇨ The above information is reprinted with kind permission from Dying Matters. Visit www.dyingmatters.org for more information.

After someone dies

An article about death, bereavement and grief for young people.

What is bereavement?

Bereavement simply means losing someone through death. It could be one of your parents, grandparents, brothers or sisters, friends, boyfriend or girlfriend – anyone who is important to you.

What might I feel?

The feelings that we have after someone close has died can be called grief. Everyone experiences grief differently – there is no 'right' way to feel. Feelings can include shock, numbness, despair, intense sadness, guilt, depression, relief, fear, anger. It can sometimes feel as if we're thrown from one feeling to another to another.

It's not unusual to feel numb, which means feeling like you have no feelings at all.

'My dad died a week ago... I'm just in a dream hoping my dad will come home but knowing he won't.'

'I feel so lost and confused, it's like all the world came crashing down, I didn't think I would ever stop crying. Now I just feel so hurt and upset.'

'Why did she have to die? I needed her. It's just not fair. Death no longer makes me sad, it makes me angry.'

'How can I cope with it all...?'

It can feel like the bottom has dropped out of your world, that nothing good will ever happen again. How can you begin to cope?

Many young people find that they can't get on with day-to-day activities. Even small things like getting out of bed, going to school, talking to friends can somehow seem enormous. Sometimes you might find that you get behind with school, college or work because you just can't concentrate. Life can just feel 'too much'. This is a common reaction. It might help to explain to someone how you're feeling – maybe a teacher you trust, a friend, someone in your family. If people know what you're going through, they are more likely to understand why you might be acting differently from normal.

'My dad died a month ago. I miss him so much, I can't cope with everyday things like going to college. I just want my dad back, is that too much to ask?'

'My mother died three years ago. I never used to speak about her. Now, I can talk about her and be proud of the time I shared with her. Whether I feel her every moment or not, I know she is always here with me.'

CRUSE BEREAVEMENT CARE

'I feel so alone...'

When you're going through something so painful, it can be hard to believe that anyone else can understand. This can lead to feeling isolated, and finding it hard to talk to friends and family.

'I feel empty, lost, confused and lonely. I need someone to talk to but don't know who.'

Although it can seem really difficult, finding someone to talk to about how you're feeling can be an important first step in coming to terms with the death of someone close. Not everyone will understand but many will. People usually like to be asked for help, so you might be surprised that your friends or family are willing to listen and to support you as best they can.

'After my sister died I got bullied because I kept crying. Things got better when I told someone.'

'The worst part is the loneliness. Nobody knows how I feel. I just wish I had someone to talk to.'

If someone in your family has died it may mean a lot of changes at home. Everyone can feel so caught up by what's going on for them individually that it can be hard to talk to each other. In fact, sharing how you're feeling can be a good way to support each other during this really difficult time.

If talking to someone you know seems too big a step, it might be easier to talk to someone whose job it is to listen.

You can ring Cruse's freephone number on 0808 808 1677 to chat to a trained helpline adviser. Or you can go to www.rd4u.org.uk to send a private e-mail to one of our trained volunteers, and read about how other young people have coped in your situation.

'I was lucky to have a teacher who really seemed to care. She made life easier by explaining to the other kids what had happened, and by being there for me when I needed it.'

'After two years I've only just learnt that when I cry and talk about things it really helps.'

What can help?

There is no magic wand to make the pain go away or to bring life back to normal. But there are things that some young people have found do help to ease the pain, and help them to come to terms with their loss.

'When he died I was really screwed up, so I wrote poems about it. I find it easier to write than to talk. If I hadn't, I wouldn't be here now.'

'I am writing this listening to a tape which I made shortly after my Mum died with songs which remind me of her. I have found this a great help when I am feeling down – I am always crying by the end of it, but I always feel better too.'

'How about getting a helium balloon with a message for her attached and letting that go? Some people find that really helpful. Or you could write her a letter and keep it just between you and her? I keep a diary where I write messages to my brother when I feel I need to, that helps me a lot.'

'I recommend that anyone in my situation should put any memories (letters, badges, I put in some dried petals from the rose I put on her coffin – anything really) into a box with a lock on. Every now and again, unlock the memory box and refresh your memory.'

'Every year on the anniversary of his death she watches his favourite film. She says she can picture him smiling and sometimes hear him laughing at his favourite bits!'

How long will it take?

Grieving is such an individual process that it's impossible to say how long it 'should' take. Feelings tend to come and go in circles, so that some people worry that they're feeling sad again, or angry, or guilty, when they thought they'd 'got over' that feeling. What most people do find, though, is that gradually, over time, things do get easier.

And remember, you are allowed to have fun and to laugh! This does not mean that you will ever forget the person who has died, or that they will be less important to you.

'Don't give yourself a time limit, everybody grieves differently and for different lengths of time. I'm still grieving for my mum after four years but in different ways. It's a long, hard journey. But what's certain is that the pain will ease gradually.'

'All I can say is be patient with yourself. There's no magic pill, no words, no secret recipe. Give yourself time! Grieve in your own time and at your own pace.'

'I feel like my mother's spirit is always near me and these things make me carry on, I love my life now, I hope you can carry on like I did.'

⇨ Information from Cruse Bereavement Care. Visit www.rd4u.org.uk for more information.

© Cruse Bereavement Care

Bereavement and young people

This information is written for and by bereaved young people, who know exactly what it is like to have someone important to them die.

What is grief?

Grief is not a disease or a sign of weakness. It is all those powerful and mixed-up feelings you have when someone you care about dies. Everyone grieves differently and there is no timetable for how long your particular grief will last. Grief affects how you feel and how you behave, but however much it hurts you will eventually feel better.

In the beginning...

'I didn't enjoy myself for ages.'

'I didn't know what to do...'

'I felt something special in my life was missing.'

'I couldn't cry.'

'I felt so lonely.'

'I felt so scared.'

Grief is not a disease or a sign of weakness. It is all those powerful and mixed-up feelings you have when someone you care about dies

---

It's OK if you feel...

- ➪ sad
- ➪ helpless
- ➪ lonely
- ➪ numb
- ➪ anxious
- ➪ tired
- ➪ awkward
- ➪ different
- ➪ confused
- ➪ relieved
- ➪ guilty
- ➪ cold
- ➪ angry

- ➪ shaky...

and it's OK if you don't.

How you might behave

You might...

- ➪ cry a lot or not at all
- ➪ want to 'go wild' to block out the pain
- ➪ have angry outbursts
- ➪ want to be on your own
- ➪ be forgetful and disorganised
- ➪ not want to go to school
- ➪ have problems eating or sleeping

What might happen

You might...

- ➪ not want to go out and have fun
- ➪ not be able to concentrate at school
- ➪ be fed up and angry with everyone
- ➪ have headaches or feel sick or unwell
- ➪ have friends who skirt around you

Moving on

Feeling better may take longer than you think but you will gradually have more good days than bad. You will never forget the person who died but will carry your memories of them wherever you are. Grief may change you but it won't destroy you.

As time goes by

'The prickles round your heart get less sharp.'

'Every anniversary hurts but as time goes by they hurt less.'

'It feels OK to have fun.'

'You begin to look forward while remembering the past too.'

'It might feel like the end of the world but trust me it isn't.'

What can help?

⇨ Talking – to anyone you feel comfortable with

⇨ Writing poetry or letters or a diary

⇨ Having a good cry

⇨ Exercising

⇨ Treating yourself

⇨ Listening to music or reading

⇨ Joining a group

⇨ Having fun with friends

⇨ Beating a cushion and shouting

⇨ Books and the web

Who can help?

⇨ SeeSaw if you're in Oxfordshire – tel: 01865 744768

⇨ Friends and family

⇨ Your doctor

⇨ Youth services

⇨ Teachers

⇨ School health nurse

⇨ Minister of your faith

⇨ Information from SeeSaw. Visit www.seesaw.org.uk for more information.

© SeeSaw

Facts and figures on child bereavement

How many children and young people are bereaved?

Bereavement in children and young people is more frequent than many people think. 78% 11- to 16-year-olds in one survey said that they had been bereaved of a close relative or friend.

Are some groups more likely to be bereaved?

Yes. Mortality rates vary by social class and geography, so it follows that children living in disadvantaged areas are more likely to be bereaved. Also, some groups of children may be more likely to experience particular kinds of bereavement: for example, mortality rates among disabled young people with complex health needs are higher than among the general population, so young people attending special school are probably more likely to be bereaved of a friend than their peers in mainstream schools.

How many children and young people are bereaved of a parent, brother or sister?

Around 1 in 29 children and young people aged five to 16 have experienced the death of a parent or sibling.

Winston's Wish, a CBN subscriber estimate that 24,000 children are bereaved of a parent each year in the UK: that is 53 children a day, or approximately one child every 22 minutes. But no-one knows the exact numbers. Data is collected each year on the number of children affected by the divorce of their parents, but not on the number affected by the death of a parent. CBN believes we need to know this information urgently, to plan for service development and to make sense of some of the research on the impact of bereavement.

How many schools are supporting bereaved children?

A survey of primary schools in Hull found that over 70% had a child on roll who had been bereaved of someone important to them in the last two years. Around 1 in 29 children All schools will be affected by bereavement at some point.

⇨ The above information is reprinted with kind permission from the Childhood Bereavement Network, hosted by NCB. Visit www.childhoodbereavementnetwork.org.uk for more information.

© NCB

SEESAW / CHILDHOOD BEREAVEMENT NETWORK

Bereaved children

How age can affect a child's understanding of death and dying.

> **Our understanding about death and dying increases with age. Broadly speaking, it follows this sort of pattern over the years from three or four to around ten:**
>
> The hamster's not moving but he'll play with me tomorrow.
>
> The hamster won't ever play again.
>
> Old people die and we can never play with them again.
>
> Grandpa may die one day in the future.
>
> Mummy and daddy will die when they're old.
>
> I will die when I'm old.
>
> Not only old people die. Mummy and daddy could die tomorrow if something happened.
>
> I could die tomorrow.

Under five or six, a child may not be able to understand that death is permanent nor that it happens to every living thing. A four-year-old may be able to tell others confidently that 'my daddy's dead' and may even be able to explain how 'he was hit by a car and he died'. However, the next sentence may be: 'I hope he'll be back before my birthday' or 'He's picking me up tonight.'

When first told of the death, younger children may be mainly concerned with the 'when' and 'where' of the death

Slightly older children may still have this hope and belief that the death will not be permanent but are beginning to understand 'forever'. Children bereaved when they are five to eight years old may feel that they can in some way reverse what has happened ('Dad will come back if I'm very good and eat my broccoli').

They may also feel – as may older children and young people – that they in some way caused the death. ('I was angry with him and shouted at him when he left for work because he wouldn't fix my bike. I refused to give him a hug. And then he never came home again. It's all my fault.') It is so common for a young person to feel they may have contributed to the death that it's worth saying

something like: 'You do know, don't you, that nothing you said or didn't say and nothing you did or didn't do made this happen?'

When first told of the death, younger children may be mainly concerned with the 'when' and 'where' of the death. Slightly older ones may also want to know the 'how' and older children and young people will also explore the 'why'.

Under five or six, a child may not be able to understand that death is permanent nor that it happens to every living thing

Younger children will express their concerns about their own future. Don't be surprised if a child asks you: 'What will happen to me? Who will meet me after school? Will I still go to Cubs?' Whatever reassurance is possible about continuing everyday activities and arrangements will be appreciated, or clear explanations given about alternative arrangements. 'At the moment, we're working all this out. What I do know is that we will still be living in this house at least until Christmas and that granny Jane will meet you from school on the days I can't. You can still have Bethany to tea whenever you want.'

As children begin to understand more about death and dying, a death in the family may make them anxious about the health and safety of surviving members of the family. Don't be surprised if the children become more clingy or more reluctant to see you leave. They may feel that they need to stick close to protect you from the mysterious occurrence that made their dad disappear or at least to be with you if it happens again. Older children may feel very responsible for you and younger siblings and feel the need to keep a close eye on your safety.

By the age of ten, children will usually have all of the bits of the jigsaw puzzle of understanding. They will even understand that they are able to cause their own death. They will appreciate clear and detailed information – beyond 'when', 'where' and 'how' the death happened, they will be interested in 'why'.

⇨ Information from Winston's Wish. Visit www.winstonswish.org.uk for more information.

© Winston's Wish

WINSTON'S WISH

We need to talk about death

Sir Al Aynsley-Green knows how it feels to lose a parent at a young age – and now he wants to help other bereaved children.

By Amol Rajan

Not many people know that every half an hour a child in Britain loses a parent. Fewer still know that the rate at which British children lose either a grandparent, close school friend, or mentor is higher still. Our ignorance of these alarming figures is partly due to the fact that no official statistics exist for the number of young people experiencing the trauma of bereavement. The above figures are simply the conservative estimates produced by an organisation known as the Childhood Bereavement Network.

Not many people know that every half an hour a child in Britain loses a parent

And yet the severity of the problem is beyond dispute. Bereavement means 'to leave desolate or alone, especially by death'. It is distinguished from grief, which means any form of deep mental anguish, by its emphasis on the solitude of those who endure it. And to a much greater extent than adults, children struggle to cope with the toxic combination of sorrow and solitude.

When married to the frequency of childhood bereavement, this presents something akin to a national disaster. It is one that the man tasked with representing children's interests to government – and we're certainly not talking

about Ed Balls, the Schools Secretary here – is beginning to take seriously.

It is a curious fact that, almost immediately upon becoming the first independent Children's Commissioner in England four years ago, Sir Al Aynsley-Green set about renaming the position to which he had ascended. The Children's Commission, which he led, an off-shoot of the 2004 Children Act, had a title unbecoming of an institution whose raison d'etre was listening to children, showing them empathy, and conveying their needs to the summit of British democracy. So the Children's Commission, a name that connotes Stalin's purges, became 11 Million, which suggests warm inclusivity (there are 11 million children in Britain). Sir Al remains the Children's Commissioner.

In riverside offices next to London Bridge, whose pastel colours and overflowing children's toys evoke the sense of a kindergarten, Sir Al has invited the *Independent* in for coffee to talk about bereavement. Given his stern visage, all square jaw and spectacles, on entering his office it's difficult not to feel like a guilty pupil reporting for the headmaster's summons. But knowledge of his distinguished previous career, in which three-and-a-half decades as a children's doctor culminated in exalted status at Great Ormond Street Hospital, works as a palliative of sorts. And when he starts talking about bereaved children, the depth of his commitment to their welfare is both tangible and poignant.

'In my clinical work I've met countless families who've lost a baby or a child through illness or trauma or whatever it may be,' he says. 'Just working with those families and often being responsible for the management of the child that died, I've always been extremely conscious of the impact on the parents – and also on the siblings.'

His 'professional experience of working with very sick babies and children and seeing the impact, what happens when a child dies', is, he says, ample qualification for a new drive to improve services for children who are bereaved. But there is a second facet to his fitness for the role, the one that draws poignancy. 'I can relate to these children very closely,' Sir Al says, 'because I was a bereaved child when my dad died unexpectedly when I was ten. I won't go into the personal circumstances but he died unexpectedly when I was ten and the impact on me, looking back on it, was very considerable indeed.'

The unforeseen tragedy was, in fact, what caused Sir Al to become a doctor. 'I have come to understand the real impact as I've grown older, and I think probably a lot of the reactions I had have been sublimated or repressed in my thinking,' he says. 'There was one very important consequence of that bereavement, which is that I decided at the age of ten I wanted to be a doctor. It changed my whole way of thinking as a child: I wanted to stop other people dying. It was a very child-like and childish feeling, but it certainly transformed my life.'

Sir Al seems, as he vocalises his experience, to still be coming to terms with its magnitude. The repression he mentions is only vaguely palpable, so it seems sensible to ask what emotions exactly he was going through back then. 'Confusion, anger, dismay. It's difficult now there's so much distance. Talking to children who've been recently bereaved, they may be very confused, they may be very angry' – his rising cadence as he says this suggests some of it may be autobiographical – 'they may feel very guilty, that they are somehow responsible for the death. They may be very tearful. They may not want to show it because they see adults who are obviously experiencing grief. There are all sorts of ways children may respond: grief is a very personal reaction, so it'll impact on their emotional health, on their physical health, it'll impact on their school ability and it may have very long-term implications.'

All doctors think about death more than lay people, because they are forced, far more than most, to confront its constant possibility. Sir Al has strong views on the censorship of discussion of death, which he feels is an impediment not only to our understanding and preparation for it, but also to helping those for whom death has become a big part of life.

'I think it's a taboo subject in our society. Death is something we don't like talking about,' he says. 'That's in stark contrast to the situation in this country 150 years ago. In Victorian times death was everywhere. Parents often expected many of their children to die and of course diseases that have disappeared now carried off countless thousands of people. So death was part of life. Now we really don't expect people to die. In medicine we try very hard to keep everyone alive.'

This, clearly, is a laudable aim. But for those people, and children especially, who are forced to confront mortality, 'death comes in all sorts of ways – expected and unexpected'. To this end, Sir Al says he is planning to make bereavement a new pillar of the 11 Million remit. He will work with voluntary organisations including Winston's Wish, Cruse and Jigsaw4U – all charities devoted to helping children cope with bereavement – to raise awareness of the issues and, to the extent that he can, help channel funds towards an under-nourished cause. 'These voluntary organisations are trying very hard to give a first-rate service,' Sir Al says, 'but it's part of the problem that some kids don't have a clue they exist.'

One of the triggers for his recently renewed interest was a documentary he'd seen about Winston's Wish, which focused on the weekend residential programmes they run for children who have suffered loss. 'One of the final clips was the sight of children where each one was given a helium balloon, and they were invited to write a message on the balloon to their loved one,' he says, clearly moved by the recollection. 'And they all released these balloons, and they disappeared as tiny specks in the sky, and that had a huge impact on me because when my father died I had not been allowed to see his body, I had not been allowed to talk about it, I was surrounded by adults who were obviously grieving and distressed and so on, and, in their kindness to me I think, they were trying to protect me. But the consequence was I really had a very unfortunate experience.'

It's a testament to him that, five-and-a-half decades on from that trauma, his work is doing much to relieve other children of a similar fate.

Learning to grieve: how children deal with loss

⇨ Children's response to death depends very much on their developmental stage. Up to the age of five, children view death as non-permanent and reversible, a product of 'magical thinking' in which the person might come back.

⇨ Children need to be given an honest, age-appropriate understanding of the circumstances of the death or separation to prevent them inventing things to fill the gaps, or even believing that they were in some way responsible. Even if these thoughts are not openly expressed, the child should be given lots of reassurance that they were in no way responsible.

⇨ Despite reassurance, many children have serious misgivings about what may happen to them or others in the family, and they need to have these fears listened to and addressed.

⇨ Children are more able to deal with stressful situations if they are given the truth and the support to deal with it. Parents should not use euphemisms to avoid the truth.

⇨ Children and young adults in ambiguous situations take their cues for appropriate behaviour from adults and every effort should be made to demonstrate how to adapt to loss by sharing your own thoughts, experiences and memories.

By Paul Bingham, an independent chartered psychologist, practising in Northamptonshire

9 June 2009

THE INDEPENDENT

Potential indicators of complicated bereavement

Information from Cruse Bereavement Care.

Complicated bereavement (also known as complicated mourning, complicated grief, prolonged grief) is the concept used when a bereaved person appears to be 'stuck' in their grief process or their grief has become a way of life.

Grief is a natural response to the death of someone close and everyone will experience grief in a unique and individual way. Although there are no limits as to how long grieving should last and what it should consist of, practitioners, healthcare professionals and academics agree that if a bereaved person is unable to move forward through their grief, then they are most likely exhibiting complicated bereavement. Both anticipated bereavement (when a person is expected to die as a result of a terminal illness) and unexpected bereavement can be further complicated for children and young people by a number of factors.

Relationship factors

The relationship that the child or young person had with the person who has died is extremely important. For example, complicated grief is more likely to occur if the person who has died was the child's parent, sibling or best friend. If the child or young person was dependent

upon the person who has died or has been diagnosed with mental health problems then the risk of complicated grief increases.

Circumstantial factors

If the death was sudden and unexpected or as a result of suicide the child or young person is at greater risk of experiencing complicated grief. The bereaved child or young person may feel responsible for not being able to prevent the death and in the case of suicide may be acutely aware of social stigma.

Multiple losses

This means that a child or young person who has experienced other deaths previously or has experienced a number of people close to them die in one instance (for example a terrorist attack, natural disaster or road traffic accident with one or more people close to the child or young person involved) are more vulnerable to complicated grief. Also, if before or after the death a child or young person has suffered other losses such as a change in school or the divorce of parents, this too can make complicated grief more likely.

> *If a bereaved person is unable to move forward through their grief, then they are most likely exhibiting complicated bereavement*

Personality factors

How emotionally resourceful or resilient a child or young person is may determine if that child or young person will experience complicated grief. If a child or young person has poor coping skills, is culturally isolated or financially deprived this can increase the likelihood of complicated grief.

Social factors

If a bereaved child or young person is exposed to poor housing, substance misuse, domestic violence and poverty they can be at risk of complicated grief. The probability of complicated grief is increased if the bereaved child or young person does not have access to social networks and appropriate support systems.

General advice

It is important to remember that not all children and young people who experience any of these factors will automatically experience complicated grief. Anyone can be at risk of complicated grief and not necessarily because of these factors.

The *British Medical Journal* has described complicated grief as, '…the persistent and disruptive yearning, pining and longing for the deceased.' The following are what the *BMJ* stated as being symptomatic of complicated grief:

1 Frequent trouble accepting the death.

2 Inability to trust others since the death.

3 Excessive bitterness related to the death.

4 Uneasiness about moving on with life.

5 Detachment from other people to whom the bereaved person was previously close.

6 The prolonged feeling that life is meaningless.

7 The view that the future will never hold any prospect of fulfilment.

8 Excessive and prolonged agitation since the death.

As the nature of grief is so individual it can be difficult to identify possible complicated grief. The process of grief can move quickly or can proceed slowly but no change at all can be worrying. An indicator of complicated grief is grief that appears to be stuck or frozen and the bereaved child or young person cannot move towards acceptance of the death. The grief becomes the child or young person's life and they can appear reluctant or anxious to progress on their journey through bereavement.

Complicated grief often requires support; therefore, if you think that a bereaved child or young person is exhibiting signs of this you may want to contact Cruse.

How can I help?

⇨ Remember that the grieving process differs from person to person and therefore complicated grief can be difficult to identify.

⇨ If you are concerned that your child or young person has become 'stuck' in their grief contact Cruse Bereavement Care for support and advice.

⇨ Encourage your child or young person to talk about their feelings and what they are thinking. Talking can help the bereaved child or young person process their grief and feel supported.

⇨ If your child or young person has mentioned taking their own life speak with your GP immediately.

⇨ Don't be embarrassed to ask for help, you are doing the right thing for your child or young person.

Key points to remember

⇨ Complicated grief occurs when the bereaved child or young person becomes stuck within their grief.

⇨ Certain factors such as the relationship the bereaved child or young person shared with the person who has died or the presence of good support systems can increase/decrease the likelihood of complicated grief.

⇨ Complicated grief can be observed when a bereaved child or young person's mourning has become the all-consuming feature of their life.

⇨ Bereaved children and young people experiencing complicated grief will require support.

⇨ Grief is a natural response to bereavement but grief that is complicated can be unhelpful and potentially damaging to the mourner.

⇨ Information from Cruse Bereavement Care. Visit www.crusebereavementcare.org.uk for more information.

© *Cruse Bereavement Care*

Top tips from bereaved children

1 Write something difficult on paper then screw it up and throw it away.

2 Write a diary about how you feel, make up poems, music and songs.

3 Talk to other people who understand how you feel, and to those who knew the person (someone in your family or close friends).

4 Put things or feelings away safely sometimes, so you can take them out another time.

5 It's OK to feel sad, angry and scared and to cry, and it is also OK to feel happy and to enjoy things.

6 Visiting the grave may make you feel closer to the person you have lost.

7 In your mind or out loud, talk to the person who has died.

8 It is OK not to have the person in your mind all the time.

9 Thinking about happy and special times spent with that person and feeling glad that you did have them in your life.

10 Having a hug.

11 Taking a deep breath.

⇨ Information from Grief Encounter. Visit www.griefencounter.org.uk for more information.

© *Grief Encounter*

Bereaved parents

The information contained in this article is provided by parents who have themselves been bereaved. Although we know that consolation is impossible, we offer you our experience at this terrible time.

How you might feel

Most people experience a whole range of different emotions; initial feelings may include disbelief, numbness, anger, sadness, guilt, emptiness, maybe even – in some instances – a sense of relief. These feelings may be mixed up together, such that you wonder if you are going mad. It is very likely that if you have other children they will also have equally strong feelings, and may need a trusted person or friend in whom to confide.

Some parents will need to talk about the child's death over again for many months. Some parents will not want to talk about it at all, and will wish to try and 'divert' their feelings, some of the time, into work and hobbies, sometimes to an obsessive extent. The greatest difficulty may be experienced where one parent needs to talk, and the other cannot listen or express their own feelings.

It is very common for partners only to have energy for their own grief and be temporarily unable to help each other. You may have to acknowledge together that you are expressing your grief in different ways, and respect each other's need to find support in your individual ways. Having someone listen to the way you feel is almost always helpful. Try not to be afraid to ask for help, outside the family if necessary, especially if you feel that your need to talk is a further 'burden' on relatives and friends.

Talking to someone you met perhaps at the hospital may be helpful, or you may find support through the hospital Social Work Department, your GP or Health Visitor, or child's teacher. There are also specialist voluntary groups and organisations for families whose child has died in particular circumstances. There may also be groups of parents, perhaps in your area, who meet through such organisations to share experience and mutual support. Some addresses of these organisations and of telephone support services are included in the Links section on this website.

As months and years go on

The numbness you felt initially will pass in time, but feelings of occasional disbelief, terrible sadness, anger, guilt and emptiness may remain very powerful. Many bereaved parents mention similar experiences.

⇨ The feeling of being on an emotional rollercoaster.

⇨ The need to talk about the child constantly.

⇨ Trying to put on a brave face for others.

⇨ The question 'Will I ever feel better?'.

⇨ The feeling that there is no point in getting up to start the day.

⇨ The feeling that no future can be envisaged – to the extent of thoughts of suicide.

⇨ The feeling of constant struggle to live hour by hour and day by day.

As at the time of your child's death, do not be afraid to ask for help; talk to someone you trust about the way you feel.

Some parents will need to talk about the child's death over again for many months. Some parents will not want to talk about it at all, and will wish to try and 'divert' their feelings

---

Anniversaries

The anticipation of anniversaries may be especially difficult, and unexpected and poignant feelings and reactions may take you by surprise.

Other people's reaction

Some people, while meaning well, may say very clumsy things. They do not mean to hurt you further, but they can have no idea of the depth of your grief.

⇨ Some may not know what to say, and say nothing at all.

⇨ Some may feel they cannot face you. They may avoid you.

⇨ Some may feel they should not mention your child, for fear of upsetting you.

⇨ Some may be frightened of the reality that they or their own children could also die, because this has happened to you.

⇨ Most will not know how to react.

- ⇨ Some people will think you should be 'over it' in a matter of months.
- ⇨ Some people may, very tactlessly, try to find something 'positive' to advise, such as focusing attention on other children you may have, or by using unhelpful clichés.

Any child born into your family in the future should know about his or her brother or sister, and be given the opportunity to ask and talk about him or her

Tell them how you want them to react. If you want them to talk about your child, and to use his or her name, tell them.

It is not uncommon for friendships, or for your circle of friends, to change in these circumstances.

Other children

Even if you have included brothers and sisters as openly as you can, their needs over months and years to talk about their brother or sister, and what happened, will change as they mature, and you may find that much basic information is required, perhaps over and over again.

Any child born into your family in the future should know about his or her brother or sister, and be given the opportunity to ask and talk about him or her.

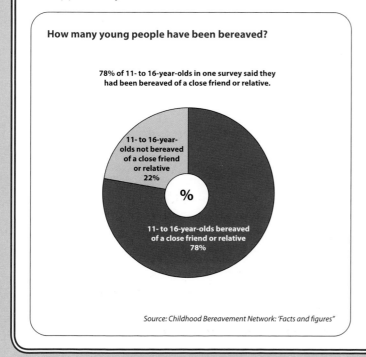

How many young people have been bereaved?

78% of 11- to 16-year-olds in one survey said they had been bereaved of a close friend or relative.

11- to 16-year-olds not bereaved of a close friend or relative 22%

%

11- to 16-year-olds bereaved of a close friend or relative 78%

Source: Childhood Bereavement Network: 'Facts and figures'

If your only child has died you may feel a desperate and bitter sadness, that your parenthood is no longer visible to others. Whether you have other children or not, if you long for another baby, but pregnancy is not possible, or does not occur, this can be an added grief.

If you are already expecting a baby, or become pregnant again soon after your bereavement, you may feel very frightened about your ability to love and care for this new baby. Alternatively, you may worry that focusing on the new baby will prevent you 'remembering' and grieving for your child who has died. You may also sometimes find yourself becoming particularly anxious about the wellbeing of this baby – or of other children you may have.

All of these feelings are normal, and you may be helped by talking about the way you feel to someone you trust.

The future

The death of your child is the most devastating thing that can happen to you. Surviving it may seem impossible for a very long time. Your life will, of course, never be the same again, but a life worth living is possible.

As you go through the rest of your life, memories and thoughts of your child will always be with you. Nearly everyone needs help in some way, so do not be afraid to ask, no matter how long it is since the death.

⇨ The above information is reprinted with kind permission from the Child Death Helpline. Visit www.childdeathhelpline.org.uk for more information.

© *Child Death Helpline*

CHILD DEATH HELPLINE

'Yes, you can survive the death of a child'

The fate of Neil and Kazumi Puttick, who committed suicide after the death of their disabled son, touched the nation. Cassandra Jardine meets a couple who lost two daughters but fought on.

Rachel and Peter Griffiths understand the suicidal thoughts that overwhelmed Neil and Kazumi Puttick who, last Sunday, threw themselves off Beachy Head, carrying their dead son's body in a rucksack. Such thoughts are common among parents whose child dies.

'Pete and I both, separately, thought about drowning ourselves,' says Rachel. 'You need to have hope for the future, and there were times when we didn't.'

The Putticks' precious only child, Sam, first suffered spinal damage in a car crash, aged one, then died suddenly, aged five, from bacterial meningitis. The Griffiths endured a different double blow: the loss of two children, Misha and Natalie, to a rare inherited condition. Shocked by the Putticks' death, Rachel is now trying to work out what got them through that infinitely painful time, in the hope that it might help others.

'You need to have hope for the future, and there were times when we didn't'

The walls of the Griffiths's home near Aylesbury, Buckinghamshire, are covered in photographs of the two enchanting little girls they have lost: Misha, who died in November 2002 just after her seventh birthday, and Natalie, whose death came a year later, just before she turned six. 'I can't remember the exact days,' says Rachel, 39. 'Mercifully, you forget so much. I prefer to celebrate their birthdays.'

Settling down with a cup of tea, waiting for Peter, a photographer, to return from a job, she starts to describe when and why she felt like ending it all: 'The first time was when we got the diagnosis; the second was before Misha died.'

Nothing in her early life had, or even could have, prepared her for the intense emotions to come. She and Peter met in their teens and married 20 years ago when she was 19 and he was 24. By the time Misha was born, six years later in 1997, Rachel was a trained nurse. 'She was born six weeks prematurely and had speech problems, but was making progress when she had her first fit, aged two-and-a-half.'

After a year of further fits and gradual regression, staff at the John Radcliffe Hospital in Oxford put the problem down to Batten's disease – a hereditary neurological condition in which cells' waste products are deposited in the brain, causing fits, loss of speech and movement and eventually death.

'All the symptoms fitted, so I feared the worst,' says Rachel. 'Even so, when they told us the results, I felt physically sick. Two weeks later, when they told us that Natalie also had the disease, it was even harder to take. I had convinced myself that she was clear because she was such a robust child.'

It seemed so unfair: the chance of two parents being carriers of the recessive gene for Late Infantile Batten's disease is one in a million. 'Misha and Nat's illness was not our fault, but we still felt guilty about bringing them into the world and not being able to find a cure for them. For the second diagnosis, Pete and I had driven to the hospital in separate cars. On the way back, we both briefly considered driving into a lake. Our children had been robbed of their future; life seemed hopeless. Instead, we sat in the pub and cried.'

She jumps up to make a cup of tea for Peter, who has joined us. They give the impression of being a united couple, but for the three years following diagnosis in January 2000, they had little time to support one another. They were too busy coping as first one child, then the other, lost the ability to walk, talk and eventually even smile.

On the kitchen table sits a Bible, but even their Christian faith was sometimes more of a problem than a help. Any parent in their situation feels abandoned by God and that can compound the grief. In the longer term, however, the support of members of the church, as well as neighbours, was invaluable. At first, however, they found it hard to accept presents of food, assistance and money.

'We didn't want the notoriety and, as a bloke, I wanted to provide for my family,' explains Peter. 'But we asked the advice of a couple whose child had had Batten's and they told us to let go of our pride and let people help us. It was the right thing to do – we had a wonderful holiday in Florida that we could never have afforded, which has left us with happy memories, and many of our best friends were made in that time.'

THE TELEGRAPH

Without the help of charities too, they could not have coped emotionally or financially because, before Misha died, they were too distraught either to work or to cope with the paperwork involved in claiming benefits. 'In this country,' says Pete, 'unless you chase, nothing is given.'

Each child had dozens of carers, who made it possible for Rachel and Peter also to spend time with their two younger children. Sophie, now nine, was born the week before Misha was diagnosed with Batten's; two years later, unplanned, Zak arrived. Fortunately, both tested negative for Batten's, and have given their parents a reason to keep going. But, at the time, coping with a dying child, with another one having fits, a toddler who was into everything and a new baby was far from 'perfect', as Rachel puts it.

'Most of the carers weren't qualified, so I or Peter had to do most of the looking after the two older children. They could do nothing for themselves, though they could hear our voices, and seemed to derive some comfort from one another.

'Teatimes were the hardest, trying to get the food. I took to putting them all to bed because I couldn't keep an eye on them when they were falling over. And life was a constant round of nappies – with four of them in them for a time. What I found most difficult about it all was feeling so isolated. I was desperate to get out of the house and missed being able to do simple things, like have a cup of coffee with a friend.

'Three years of it broke me physically. I think that was why I became suicidal again for six weeks before Misha died. It was largely sleep deprivation. We didn't want to leave her alone for a minute as she was fitting constantly, so Pete sat up with her until 4am, and then I took over.'

Counselling, rather than medication, got her through. But after Misha died, they were too busy to grieve properly for her. All that was stored up for a year later when Natalie also died. Nothing can lessen the pain, but the Griffiths feel that – unlike the Putticks – they survived those first few terrible days of bereavement partly because of Helen House, the children's hospice in Oxford. The hospice helped them throughout those agonising three years, and when the girls died, helped them to come to terms with their loss. Although Natalie died at home, her body was then placed in a special room at the hospice, surrounded by her toys. 'We could say our goodbyes slowly,' says Peter. 'It also helped that we put her in the coffin ourselves.'

Even so, the change in their lives was horribly abrupt. 'Some people say they can't get the equipment out of the house fast enough, but for us the hoists and food pumps were symbols of our little girls and they were gone in 48 hours,' says Pete. 'I remember hanging on to a gastrostomy tube that had been Misha's. It was like an umbilical cord to me.

'It was hard for the younger children, too. Suddenly all the carers who they were used to spending time with were no longer there.'

As often happens, Rachel and Peter found themselves not united but divided by their different ways of grieving. 'I wanted to talk about it a lot,' Peter says. 'Rachel was more private: she felt that if she opened up, she would never be able to put the lid back on. And then there was the bedroom. I'm a typical man. I wanted physical comfort, but Rachel couldn't bear the idea.'

Peter sought refuge in the pub, where he wanted to scream when his friends chatted about football while all he wanted to talk about was his girls. Their marriage might have foundered had it not been for counselling from the Child Bereavement Charity. 'In a safe place, without the children around, we could talk about personal issues,' says Rachel.

Talking of other parents who had been through similar pain also made them feel less alone. 'They made us believe,' says Peter, 'that there is light not just at the end of the tunnel, but in the middle of it.'

But, of course, their greatest ballast against despair came from having two needy younger children. 'It's much harder if you have lost your only child, like the Putticks,' says Rachel. 'Some of the other parents in our bereavement groups were in that situation, and they too eventually found ways of coping. We didn't want just to give in to the despair.'

One common way is to help others. As soon as she was able, Rachel started work as a nurse at Douglas House, the brother organisation to Helen House which helps dying 16- to 35-year-olds and their families. She also provides respite foster care – but nothing can assuage the loss of their two precious girls.

There are still days, she says, when they feel as bad as they did immediately after their daughters' deaths, but they have found a way of comforting themselves. 'One of the hopes you have for your children is that they will have a positive impact on others during their lives. We know that many people were inspired by knowing Misha and Nat, so those hopes were fulfilled. It doesn't matter so much how long their lives were.'

Sadly, Neil and Kazumi Puttick gave in to despair before they could find something to celebrate in their son's short but joyous life.

⇨ For more information or to support the work of the Child Bereavement Charity, call 01494 446648 or visit www.childbereavement.org.uk

7 June 2009

What can I do to plan for my death?

Most of us avoid the subject of death – it isn't generally considered to be polite conversation and it certainly can dampen the mood. Plus, most of us think that we still have plenty of time, and prefer to cross that bridge when we come to it. But, a bit of planning and communication with your loved ones now could mean avoiding a lot of heartache for them later.

What makes a 'good' death?

Is the idea of a 'good' death a contradiction in terms? To answer that, try thinking about your idea of a bad death. Would it include pain, confusion, discomfort, loneliness, and inability to communicate your wishes? Well, you could help to avoid all of those things by planning a little now, whether you are ill or not, and whatever your age.

It can often help to begin by talking to those close to you about death because it can help you realise what's important to you, and to them. Some things to consider are:

⇨ who you would like to be with you if you were close to death,

⇨ where you would like to be – such as a hospice, at home, or in a hospital,

⇨ whether you want to know, or want your family to know, when you are close to death,

⇨ who would be the person to tell others that you are soon to die,

⇨ who would be responsible for making decisions about your care on your behalf, that could not be made by you in advance, and

⇨ how you would want your final days to sound and look – such as your favourite music, TV programmes, or flowers.

Write down your wishes and make sure someone knows where they are, just in case they're needed. Remember, you can update it as often as you like, and your loved ones will undoubtedly be happy to know exactly what will make you feel as comfortable as possible when the inevitable happens. You can also write down what you would like at your funeral, so that your family can carry out your wishes.

Let's get practical

You may not feel like being practical about your own death – let's face it, you won't be worrying about how tidy your filing system is when your time's up. But for your family, your messy files and unorganised finances could be a living nightmare. Plus, if you haven't written a will, things can get even more confusing.

When a loved one dies, it can be very hard coping with practical issues on top of the sadness, grief and sometimes, shock. So, take some time to get your affairs in order – it might not be as time consuming as you think – and you'll probably feel comfortable knowing everything's organised.

Things to get sorted include:

⇨ Your will – a 'DIY' package for straightforward wills is the cheapest method, but you do miss out on face-to-face advice. Asking a lawyer to do it for you costs a bit more, but it can be worth it, especially if you have more complicated requirements. Visit The Law Society website for guidance on writing a will (see 'further information'), and lawyers in your area.

⇨ Your financial details – after your death your next of kin will need to know about your bank accounts, savings accounts, mortgage, credit cards, pension, and any other financial contracts. Having a list handy, which you update as things change, makes it a lot easier.

⇨ Important documents – they'll also need to know where you keep important documents like the deeds to your house, your passport, insurance policies, and birth and marriage certificates.

15 January 2009

⇨ Reproduced from NHS Choices with permission.

NHS CHOICES

Why make a will?

Information from HM Court Services.

This information applies to the law of England and Wales only. It is not intended to be legal advice, nor a substitute for seeking appropriate professional advice about the disposal of your assets. Probate Service staff are not able to give advice on whether you should make a will, nor its contents.

Wills

People do not like thinking about death and the effects it has on those they leave behind, but it is something that has to be faced eventually. It is natural that you should wish your property and assets to pass on your death to whomever you choose. By making a will you can ensure that your assets go to those you wish should have them.

There are some assets that cannot be given away in your will (e.g. property you hold in joint names usually passes automatically to the other joint owner) but most of your property can be dealt with by a will.

What is a will?

It is a legal declaration of how you wish to dispose of your property on your death. In order for it to be valid it must comply with certain requirements.

Who can make a will?

Generally speaking, anyone over the age of 18 and of sound mind.

However:

⇨ It is possible for members of the armed forces to make a will under the age of 18 but legal advice should be sought in these circumstances.

⇨ Under the provisions of the Mental Health Act 1983, the Court of Protection may approve the making of a will, or a codicil to a will for someone who is mentally incapable of doing so themselves. Guidance about how a mentally incapable person can make a will or codicil can be obtained from the Public Guardianship Office website.

What makes a will valid?

⇨ It must be in writing, should appoint someone to carry out the instructions (an executor) and dispose of possessions/property.

⇨ It must be signed by the person making the will (the testator), or signed on the testator's behalf in his or her presence and by his or her direction. This must be done in the presence of two witnesses who then sign the will in the presence of the testator.

Who can be a witness?

Anyone who:

⇨ is not blind;

⇨ is capable of understanding the nature and effect of what they are doing.

However, a witness should not be:

⇨ a beneficiary in the will; or

⇨ married to, or be the civil partner of, a beneficiary.

In these circumstances the will remains a valid and legal document, but the gift to the beneficiary cannot be paid.

> **Example:**
>
> Sally is an 83-year-old widow. She doesn't have any children and her only living relative, her sister Maria, lives in Australia. Sally gets on really well with her neighbours, Kate and Sue and wants to leave them something when she dies. Sally instructs a solicitor to draft her will splitting her estate equally between Kate and Sue.
>
> Once Sally has approved the will, she makes her own arrangements for the will to be signed and witnessed. Sally knows that neither Kate nor Sue should witness her will. However, she doesn't know that Kate and Sue's husbands, David and Simon, should not witness the will either. Consequently, David and Simon witness the will.
>
> When Sally dies the gifts to Kate and Sue will fail because their husbands witnessed the will and Sally's estate will pass under the intestacy rules (the rules which apply where there is no will or no valid will).

Intestacy rules

What happens if a will is not valid?

It is disregarded and the deceased person's property is distributed in accordance with the intestacy rules.

What if I don't make a will?

If you don't leave a valid will your estate will pass in accordance with the intestacy rules. The intestacy rules set out who is entitled to inherit from your estate if you don't leave a valid will.

If you are married or are in a civil partnership, the first person entitled to your estate under the intestacy rules is your spouse/civil partner, but he or she will not

HER MAJESTY'S COURT SERVICE

Organic donation

Information from ifishoulddie.co.uk

Every so often, the desperate need for organ donors is highlighted in the national press and this difficult subject is brought to the nation's attention. Once again, it is a very personal decision, but certainly one you should discuss with your immediate family, and at least make your views known.

NHS Blood and Transplant (NHSBT) was established as a Special Health Authority in England and Wales in October 2005 with responsibilities across the United Kingdom in relation to organ transplantation. Its remit is to provide a reliable, efficient supply of blood, organs and associated services to the NHS.

There are currently just over 14 million registered organ donors in the UK (23% of the population) who have said they want to help others live after their death by joining the NHS Organ Donor Register. UK Transplant has unveiled plans to increase organ transplant numbers to new levels as part of the NHSBT's strategy.

The generosity of donors and their families enables nearly 3,000 people in the UK every year to take on a new lease of life. It is now possible to use all the major organs (heart, kidneys, lungs, liver, pancreas and small bowel) in transplantation and so one donor is able to help many other people.

Cornea transplantation is one of medicine's big success stories and is one of the most commonly performed transplant operations with a very good success rate, helping more than 2,000 blind and partially-sighted people. However, the shortage of donated corneas means that many more people could be given the opportunity to see again if there were more donors.

⇨ If the death happened in hospital, staff may ask for permission to use organs for transplantation.

Next we'll hear from all those John has helped after his death...

Many people find such an approach difficult in the early stages of bereavement but organs have to be removed very soon after death.

⇨ Other organs such as corneas and heart valves can be removed anything up to 72 hours after death.

⇨ If death occurs at home or somewhere other than a hospital, organs other than the corneas cannot usually be used.

⇨ Organs will not be removed without the consent of the relatives, which is why it is worthwhile making your wishes known beforehand. This also helps save relatives from the distress of making a decision without the relevant information.

The national donor register is designed to help hospitals identify and approach grieving families. When transplant teams know the intentions of the deceased, only one per cent of families refuse to allow organs to be taken, compared to 30 per cent when intentions are not known. Apparently, the national donor register was only searched 20 times last year by hospitals, which is another reason for the Government's initiative.

Contact www.uktransplant.org.uk and sign up on line to the NHS Organ Donor Register or contact 0845 60 60 400 and discuss your wishes with your relatives if you do wish to donate your organs.

UK Transplant
Communications Directorate
Fox Den Road
Stoke Gifford
Bristol BS34 8RR
enquiries@uktransplant.nhs.uk
Tel: 0117 975 7575 Fax: 0117 975 7577

You can also find further information at BODY, the British Organ Donor Society at http://body.orpheusweb.co.uk/ and www.nhs.uk

The UK National Kidney Federation is run by and for kidney donors at www.kidney.org.uk

The Live Life Then Give Life campaign has been created to raise awareness of organ donation and the chronic lack of organ donors in the UK. It aims to encourage people to show their support for organ donation by wearing one of two tee shirts that have been produced especially for the campaign – www.livelifethengivelife.co.uk

To donate blood, please call The National Blood Service on 0845 7 711 711 or visit www.blood.co.uk

⇨ Information from ifishoulddie.co.uk. Visit www.ifishoulddie.co.uk for more.

© ifishoulddie.co.uk (Kate Burchill)

Practical things you may need to do after a death

Information from Cancer Research UK.

Cultural rituals and practices

In some cultures there are specific rituals and practices that are carried out after someone's death. It is important for you to do whatever you feel is right. You are likely to feel very shocked, even if you were well prepared and had been expecting it to happen. In most cases there is no need to do anything straight away. You can just stay with your friend's or relative's body for a while. You may want to have someone there to support you.

What you need to do soon after someone dies

Some things need to be done fairly quickly after the death and you may not know where to start. We hope this information helps to make the early days after the death as easy as possible.

If your relative or friend dies in hospital or a hospice, you may find after you leave that you would like to see them again. If you want to, you can arrange to visit by contacting the ward staff. They will arrange for you to see the body in the mortuary. There are rooms in the mortuary specifically for this. You will be in a small private room and be able to spend some time alone with your friend or relative. If you have certain religious needs, most mortuaries will be able to help you with these.

If your loved one dies at home you will have as much time as you want to be with them after they die. You will need to contact the GP and the funeral director and let them know that your loved one has died. After some time, the funeral director or district nurse will wash and dress your relative's body. You can help them to do this if you like. The process is different in different cultures and religions. But usually the body is carefully washed and dried, the eyelids are closed and the mouth is supported shut. The person's hair is tidied and sometimes washed. You can keep the body at home until the funeral if you like. But if the body is taken away and you feel you want to see them again before the funeral, you can arrange this with the funeral directors.

If your relative died in a hospital or hospice you will most likely need to go and collect their personal belongings. Most people find this hard but the ward staff will be supportive and very aware of your feelings. If your loved one had any valuables such as watch, jewellery or money in the ward safe, just check that the nurses have remembered to include these in their belongings. Or if there are certain items you want to remain with your loved one, such as a wedding ring, you will need to make sure you let the staff know.

Soon after the death, the next of kin needs to make an appointment with the Patient Affairs Officer. At this appointment you will collect the medical certificate with the cause of death written on it. Doctors call this a 'death certificate'. If your relative died at home, your GP will give you the form or you may need to collect it from the surgery the next day. The form tells you how to register the death.

Registering the death

It is a legal requirement to register all deaths within 5 days in England and Wales, and within eight days in Scotland. You have to register the death before you can complete the funeral arrangements. The hospital or your GP will let you know where the nearest registry office is. You must register the death in the district where the person died. You don't have to pay for registration.

Practically, the procedure is usually pretty straightforward. But it can be very upsetting for some people, so you may want to take someone to support you. If there are special situations, such as a post-mortem, registering a death may involve more paperwork and may take a bit longer.

A relative is the best person to register the death. If this isn't possible, someone else can do it but you will need to discuss this with the registry office.

You will need to take with you:

⇨ The death certificate.

⇨ The full name, address, date and place of birth and the occupation of the person who has died.

⇨ Information about their pension or other income from public funds.

⇨ If the person was married you will need to give the full name and date of birth of the surviving partner.

Once they complete these details the Registrar will give you a certificate for burial or cremation, depending on what you decide to do. You will need to give this certificate to the funeral director so they can complete the funeral arrangements. This certificate is free of charge but you will need to pay a small fee for a certified copy. You will need this copy for any bank or insurance issues or if you want to bury your friend or relative abroad.

The comfort of memorial websites

Online tributes allow us to grieve for friends, family, pets and even celebrities in public. But are they a good idea?

By Emine Saner

Most of the people who left messages this week on online memorial sites, expressing their disbelief, sorrow and grief, had never met Georgia Rowe or Neve Lafferty, the two girls who killed themselves on Sunday night. Only a few hours after the news that their bodies had been found in the River Clyde came through, memorial websites had already been created.

Memorial websites are sites where friends and family members upload photographs, sometimes videos and favourite music tracks, with space for people to leave their memories and messages of condolence. Many sites are not private and can be viewed, and added to, by anyone.

As well as messages that have been left on their profiles at social networking site Bebo, tribute pages for Rowe and Lafferty have been created on other specialist memorial sites, including Friends at Rest, Gone Too Soon and Lasting Tribute. More messages have been left in the comments field of stories about their deaths on local newspapers' sites.

> **Memorial websites are sites where friends and family members upload photographs, sometimes videos and favourite music tracks, with space for people to leave their memories and messages of condolence**

On Friends at Rest, someone called Karen Peters writes to Rowe: 'God bless sweetheart. I didn't know you that well but I can only begin to imagine what you must have been going through.' And on Lafferty's page, Jeremy Gibson writes: 'You were so young and it was such a tragic end to your life. I was so sorry to hear about your story. I hope you have finally found peace.' Their pictures sit alongside 'featured celebrity memorials'. Prominent are Patrick Swayze and Michael Jackson.

The blossoming of memorial websites is a relatively new phenomenon. 'I think there were two things that happened,' says Jonathan Davies, who founded memorial site Much Loved. 'The death of Diana brought about a change in how we grieve publicly, and then the Internet connected people and provided a place for it. Two or three years ago, when we launched, we were quite unusual.' Now there are lots of host sites, he points out, as well as families and friends starting their own pages.

Davies set up his site, which currently has around 12,000 memorials, in 2007, 12 years after his brother died suddenly at the age of 21. 'It was a drugs-related death and I think this was one of the reasons why his friends didn't get in touch with our family – there was a police investigation, and I think his friends were worried about how we would react, which led to this wall of silence,' he says. 'I think that actually made our grieving period worse. I felt a website would have opened up the channels of communication.'

Respondents were asked: 'To what extent would you support or oppose a system where people were presumed to want to donate organs unless they, or after death their family, said otherwise?' Results by gender.

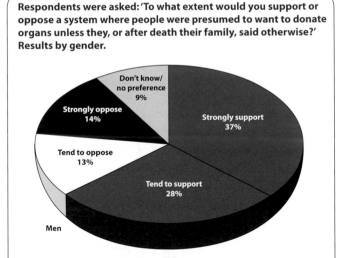

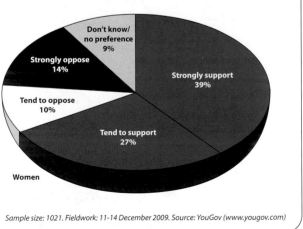

Sample size: 1021. Fieldwork: 11-14 December 2009. Source: YouGov (www.yougov.com)

Bereavement

To experience a loss; the loss of a loved on[...]
their death.

Cemetery/graveyard

Area of land where bodies are buried (unless [...]
and headstones erected to remember the dead. [...]
found attached to a place of worship or crem[...]

Cremation

A method of disposing of a dead body by bu[...]
ashes produced are given to the family of the [...]
who can either keep them or choose to sca[...]
often in a favourite place of the deceased.

Coroner

A doctor or lawyer responsible for investigati[...]

Eulogy

A speech delivered at a funeral, praising the p[...]
has died and reminiscing about their life.

Executor

Someone responsible for the administration of [...]
estate after their death, usually nominate[...]
deceased in their will.

Funeral

A ceremony, often faith-based and held in [...]
worship, which friends and family of the dece[...]
attend as a way of saying goodbye to their lo[...]

Grief

An intense feeling of sorrow felt after a bereave[...]
process of facing the loss of someone you lo[...]

Headstone

Also known as a tombstone or gravestone[...]
monument erected to a dead person, usually[...]

He believes other families gain comfort from memorial sites. 'People thought it was a bit morbid, and I suppose in a sense it is, but in a good way. Some people set up memorials very soon after someone's death – it is a way of coming to terms with what has happened, and a way to express anger and grief and a place for other family members to express condolences. We get a lot set up for young babies, or babies who died at birth, which is a way for parents to create something tangible.'

Does it say something about us as a society, that something so private as grief is now often done so publicly? 'I do think grief is becoming embraced more by communities – by that I mean people outside the immediate family. I remember in the mid-90s, when my brother died, people would ignore us because they didn't know what to say. That's beginning to change now.'

The popularity of online memorials is probably down to the convenience of leaving a message on a website rather than going out, buying flowers, writing a card and leaving it in a place where other people have done the same, as people did in such massive numbers after the death of Diana or of Holly Wells and Jessica Chapman in Soham. If our private lives are more public than ever, thanks partly to Twitter, Facebook and numerous other social networking sites, so it is with our deaths.

But is this outpouring of grief, often for celebrities, but also for those in the news, such as Lafferty and Rowe, people the mourners might never have met, actually genuine? 'It is, absolutely,' says clinical psychologist Oliver James, 'because they are talking about themselves. What is happening is that instead of gaining insight, they are acting out. Instead of properly apprehending their own difficulties, a large proportion of the people who leave these messages are identifying with the difficulties of someone else and emoting. Although the feeling is authentic and truly felt, there is a histrionic dimension to it.'

Much Loved is run as a registered charity, aimed at helping families to set up their own sites, but you can't escape the feeling that other sites might have more cynical motives. On Lasting Tribute, which is owned by the Daily Mail newspaper group, there is a shop where you can buy personalised candles, benches and jewellery. For £1, you can also leave a virtual 'gift' on people's pages – these include pictures of teddy bears, flags, a pint of beer or a heart. The site set up for Georgia Rowe – which, at the time of writing did not have any tributes, includes a link to the local newspaper's report on her death. A newspaper owned by the Daily Mail group.

You can get all your printing done – bookmarks, cards, memorial keyrings and magnets – through Gone Too Soon, which also features adverts for holiday cottages and genealogists. Its administrators add tribute pages for celebrities such as Patrick Swayze (which has attracted nearly 500 tributes), and Keith Floyd, as soon as they die. The site encourages people to set up memorials, making it clear that you don't have to be a close friend or relation. 'Don't think it's not your place to set up a site. You would not be encroaching on other family members' territory,' it writes. Proceeds from the virtual 'gifts', also £1 each, contribute to running the site.

The site probably does bring comfort to bereaved families, though it also encourages people to set up pages for pets – which doesn't sit entirely comfortably with memorials to stillborn babies. Isn't all this public grieving, and the voyeuristic nature of it, all a bit mawkish? 'You could say the same about people walking around graveyards looking at headstones, or leaving flowers at the spot where someone has died,' says Davis. 'But as long as it is done in the right way – and a memorial website can be – then it provides a time for reflection.'

⇨ Samaritans 08457 90 90 90

7 October 2009

THE GUARDIAN

KEY FACTS

⇨ Bereavement is our experience of gr[...] someone we care about has died. It isn't just o[...] but a range of different emotions. We feel the[...] the months – often up to two years, sometim[...] – after the death. (page 1)

⇨ Grieving is a natural process that can t[...] after any kind of loss. Dealing with loss ca[...] distressing but it is normal – albeit very dif[...] painful – to experience very strong reactions. [...] an illness. Your feelings are something you e[...] and not symptoms that have to be treated. ([...]

⇨ Family times such as Christmas and birthd[...] as anniversaries of the death are a particular[...] and traumatic time for a bereaved person an[...] be treated with sensitivity, particularly the first[...] they come around. (page 5)

⇨ Carers often feel grief even though th[...] they're caring for is still alive. This could hap[...] person being cared for has a life-limiting co[...] condition that has no reasonable hope of a[...] their personality has been affected by the[...] (page 6)

⇨ New research, commissioned by the Dyin[...] Coalition, shows that less than a third (29%)[...] have discussed their wishes around dying. ([...]

⇨ Bereavement in children and young peop[...] frequent than many people think. 78% of 11- t[...] olds in one survey said that they had been be[...] a close relative or friend. (page 12)

⇨ Under five or six, a child may not be able to u[...] that death is permanent nor that it happens to e[...] thing. (page 13)

⇨ Children need to be given an honest, age-a[...] understanding of the circumstances of the[...] separation to prevent them inventing things[...] gaps, or even believing that they were in s[...] responsible. (page 15)

⇨ Complicated bereavement (also known[...] plicated mourning, complicated grief, prolon[...] is the concept used when a bereaved perso[...] to be 'stuck' in their grief process or their[...] become a way of life. (page 16)

Additional Resources

Other Issues titles

If you are interested in researching further some of the issues raised in *Bereavement and Grief*, you may like to read the following titles in the *Issues* series:

⇨ Vol. 190 *Coping with Depression* (ISBN 978 1 86168 541 4)

⇨ Vol. 159 *An Ageing Population* (ISBN 978 1 86168 452 3)

⇨ Vol. 152 *Euthanasia and the Right to Die* (ISBN 978 1 86168 439 4)

⇨ Vol. 148 *Religious Beliefs* (ISBN 978 1 86168 421 9)

⇨ Vol. 147 *The Terrorism Problem* (ISBN 978 1 86168 420 2)

⇨ Vol. 136 *Self-Harm* (ISBN 978 1 86168 388 5)

⇨ Vol. 135 *Coping with Disability* (ISBN 978 1 86168 387 8)

For a complete list of available *Issues* titles, please visit our website: www.independence.co.uk/shop

Useful organisations

You may find the websites of the following organisations useful for further research:

⇨ **British Humanist Association:** www.humanism.org.uk

⇨ **Cancer Research UK:** www.cancerhelp.org.uk

⇨ **Child Bereavement Charity:** www.childbereavement.org.uk

⇨ **Childhood Bereavement Network:** www.childhoodbereavementnetwork.org.uk

⇨ **Child Death Helpline:** www.childdeathhelpline.org.uk

⇨ **Cruse Bereavement Care:** www.rd4u.org.uk

⇨ **Dying Matters:** www.dyingmatters.org

⇨ **Grief Encounter:** www.griefencounter.org.uk

⇨ **ifishoulddie:** www.ifishoulddie.co.uk

⇨ **Marie Curie Cancer Care:** www.mariecurie.org.uk

⇨ **NHS Choices:** www.nhs.uk

⇨ **Parentline Plus:** www.parentlineplus.org.uk

⇨ **Royal College of Psychiatrists:** www.rcpsych.ac.uk

⇨ **SeeSaw:** www.seesaw.org.uk

⇨ **Social Policy Research Unit, University of York:** www.york.ac.uk/spru

⇨ **Winston's Wish:** www.winstonswish.org.uk

For more book information, visit our website...

www.independence.co.uk

Information available online includes:

✓ Detailed descriptions of titles

✓ Tables of contents

✓ Facts and figures

✓ Online ordering facilities

✓ Log-in page for Issues Online (an Internet resource available free to Firm Order Issues subscribers – ask your librarian to find out if this service is available to you)

ACKNOWLEDGEMENTS

The publisher is grateful for permission to reproduce the following material.

While every care has been taken to trace and acknowledge copyright, the publisher tenders its apology for any accidental infringement or where copyright has proved untraceable. The publisher would be pleased to come to a suitable arrangement in any such case with the rightful owner.

Chapter One: Bereavement and Loss

Bereavement: key facts, © Royal College of Psychiatrists, *Bereavement – what can you do to help yourself,* © ParentlinePlus, *Coping with your grief,* © Marie Curie Cancer Care, *Helping the bereaved,* © ifishoulddie.co.uk (Kate Burchill), *Grief before death,* © Crown copyright is reproduced with the permission of Her Majesty's Stationery Office, *A stiff upper lip is no longer a badge of honour,* © The Times and 12/11/2009 / nisyndication, *Major new survey reveals people's reluctance to discuss own death,* © Dying Matters.

Chapter Two: Grief and Young People

After someone dies, © Cruse Bereavement Care, *Bereavement and young people,* © SeeSaw, *Facts and figures on child bereavement,* © NCB, *Bereaved children,* © Winston's Wish, *We need to talk about death,* © The Independent, *Potential indicators of complicated bereavement,* © Cruse Bereavement Care, *Top tips from bereaved children,* © Grief Encounter, *Bereaved children more likely to have faced other difficult events in childhood,* © NCB, *Childhood bereavement [graph],* © NCB, *Issues for bereaved children and young people,* © Childhood Bereavement Network, *Bereaved parents,* © Child Death Helpline, *How many young people have been bereaved? [graph],* © Childhood Bereavement Network, *'Yes, you can survive the death of a child',* © Telegraph Media Group Limited 2010.

Chapter Three: Handling the Formalities

What can I do to plan for my death?, © Crown copyright is reproduced with the permission of Her Majesty's Stationery Office, *Why make a will?,* © Crown copyright is reproduced with the permission of Her Majesty's Stationery Office, *Organ donation,* © ifishoulddie.co.uk (Kate Burchill), *Practical things you may need to do after a death,* © Cancer Research UK, *'Would you be willing to donate your organs after you die?' [graph],* © YouGov, *Dealing with financial companies and organisations after someone dies,* © Savvy Woman, *Financial implications of death of a partner,* © University of York, *Religious traditions and beliefs,* © ifishoulddie. co.uk (Kate Burchill), *Living funerals,* © ifishoulddie.co.uk (Kate Burchill), *Humanist funerals and memorials,* © British Humanist Association, *The comfort of memorial websites,* © Guardian News and Media Limited 2009, *'To what extent would you support or oppose a system where people were presumed to want to donate organs?' [graph],* © YouGov.

Illustrations

Pages 1, 16, 28, 31: Angelo Madrid; pages 9, 27, 32, 37: Simon Kneebone; pages 11, 18, 39a, 39b: Don Hatcher; pages 14, 21: Bev Aisbett.

Cover photography

Left: © Jean Carneiro. Centre: © Glenda Otero. Right: © jenny w.

Additional acknowledgements

Research by Claire Owen on behalf of Independence.

With thanks to the Independence team: Mary Chapman, Sandra Dennis and Jan Sunderland.

Lisa Firth
Cambridge
May, 2010